Contents

Baby guinea pigs

Guinea pigs are born with teeth and fur. Their eyes are open when they are born. Baby guinea pigs are called piglets.

Let's Read About Pets

Guinea Pigs

JoAnn Early Macken

Reading consultant: Susan Nations

W
FRANKLIN WATTS

First UK hardback edition 2004
First UK paperback edition 2005

Franklin Watts
96 Leonard Street
London EC2A 4XD

Franklin Watts Australia
45-51 Huntley Street
Alexandria
NSW 2015

ISBN 0 7496 5760 X (hardback)
ISBN 0 7496 5827 4 (paperback)

Published in association with Weekly Reader Early Learning Library, Milwaukee.

Printed in Hong Kong, China

A guinea pig's fur

Guinea pigs can have short fur or long fur. Some have fur that is silky and shiny. Some have stripes or spots in their fur.

Rough fur

Some guinea pigs have rough coats. Their fur grows in patterns that look like circles.

Teeth

Like mice, rats and gerbils, guinea pigs are rodents. Their teeth always keep growing.

Chewing

Guinea pigs like to chew on things. If you let your guinea pig loose, watch your tables and chairs! Can you guess why?

Eating and drinking

Guinea pigs need the right food to stay healthy. They can eat flakes or pellets of food. They like carrots, apples and oranges. They also need fresh water.

A guinea pig's hutch

A guinea pig can live in a hutch or a cage. Cover the bottom with wood shavings and hay.

Happy or angry?

Happy guinea pigs gurgle and jump. If you hear teeth clicking, be careful! An angry guinea pig might bite.

Running around

Guinea pigs need to run around. In good weather, they can go outside and eat grass. But watch them: guinea pigs like to hide!

New words

hutch — a pen or cage for an animal

patterns — designs

pellets — small pieces of food

rodents — small animals that gnaw, such as mice or squirrels

How to find out more

Here are a few useful websites about guinea pigs:

www.petplanet.co.uk/petplanet/kids/kidsguineapig.htm
Includes information on what your guinea pig needs, how to prepare for its arrival and a shopping list for your guinea pig

www.echobusiness.co.uk/the_north_east/petscorner/advice/guineapigs/index.html
Up-to-date questions and answers on everything to do with guinea pigs

www.abc.net.au/creaturefeatures/facts/guineapigs.htm
Useful facts on guinea pigs

> **Note** We strongly advise that Internet access is supervised by a responsible adult.

Index

Notes for teachers and parents

This book is specially designed to support the young reader in the reading process. The familiar topic is appealing to young children and invites them to read — and re-read — the book again and again. The full-colour photographs and enhanced text help the child during the reading process. After children develop fluency with the text and content, the book can be read independently.